NAPOLEON'S MAXIMS OF WAR

This work is a piece of history and, as such, may reflect events, language, and values that are different from modern sensibilities and may cause offense. Reader discretion is advised.

This book is excerpted from the 1862 "Officer's Manual" edition of "Napoleon's Maxims of War," based on Charles George D'Aguilar's 1831 translation of Napoleon's , which is in the public domain. No copyright claim is made with respect to public domain works.

This work reflects minor editorial revisions to the original text.

Cover design created using Canva.com and reproduced pursuant to its free media license agreement. Cover art derived from a Bust of Napoleon, after a model by Antonio Canova, circa 1808-1814, courtesy of the Metropolitan Museum of Art, pursuant to his public domain open access license.

No part of this book may be reproduced in any form or by any electronic or mechanical means, including information storage and retrieval systems, without written permission from the publisher, except for the use of brief quotations in a book review.

NAPOLEON'S MAXIMS OF WAR

NAPOLEON BONAPARTE

Translated by
GEORGE CHARLES D'AGUILAR

I

The frontiers of states are either large rivers, or chains of mountains, or deserts. Of all these obstacles to the march of an army, the most difficult to overcome is the desert; mountains come next, and broad rivers occupy the third place.

2

In forming the plan of a campaign, it is requisite to foresee everything the enemy may do, and to be prepared with the necessary means to counteract it.

Plans of campaign may be modified *ad infinitum* according to circumstances—the genius of the general, the character of the troops, and the topography of the theatre of action.

3

An army which undertakes the conquest of a country, has its two wings resting either upon neutral territories, or upon great natural obstacles, such as rivers or chains of mountains. It happens in some cases that only one wing is so supported; and in others that both are exposed.

In the first instance cited, viz., where both wings are protected, a general has only to protect his front from being penetrated. In the second, where one wing only is supported, he should rest upon the supported wing. In the third, where both wings are exposed, he should depend upon a central formation, and never allow the different corps under his command to depart from this: for if it be difficult to contend with the disadvantage of having *two* flanks exposed, the inconvenience is doubled by having *four*, trebled if there be *six*—that is to say, if the army is divided into two or three different corps. In the first instance, then, as above quoted, the line of operation may rest indifferently on the right or on the left. In the second, it should be directed toward the wing in support. In the third, it should be perpendicular to the centre of the army's line of march. But in all these cases it is necessary, at a distance of every five or six days march, to have a strong post or an entrenched position upon the line of operation, in order to collect military stores and provisions, to organize convoys, to form of it a centre of movement, and establish a point of defence to shorten the line of operation of the army.

4

When the conquest of a country is undertaken by two or three armies, which have each their separate line of operation, until they arrive at a point fixed upon for their concentration, it should be laid down as a principle, that the union of these different corps should never take place near the enemy; because the enemy, in uniting his forces, may not only prevent this junction, but may beat the armies in detail.

※ 5 ※

All wars should be governed by certain principles, for every war should have a definite object, and be conducted according to the rules of art. (A war should only be undertaken with forces proportioned to the obstacles to be overcome.)

6

At the commencement of a campaign, to *advance* or *not to advance*, is a matter for grave consideration; but when once the offensive has been assumed, it must be sustained to the last extremity. However skilful the manœuvres in a retreat, it will always weaken the *morale* of an army, because, in losing the chances of success, these last are transferred to the enemy. Besides, retreats always cost more men and *materiel* than the most bloody engagements; with this difference, that in a battle the enemy's loss is nearly equal to your own—whereas in a retreat the loss is on your side only.

7

An army should be ready every day, every night, and at all times of the day and night, to oppose all the resistance of which it is capable. With this view, the soldier should always be furnished completely with arms and ammunition; the infantry should never be without its artillery, its cavalry, and its generals; and the different divisions of the army should be constantly in a state to support, to be supported, and to protect itself.

The troops, whether halted, or encamped, or on the march, should be always in favorable positions, possessing the essentials required for a field of battle; for example, the flanks should be well covered, and all the artillery so placed as to have free range, and to play with the greatest advantage. When an army is in column of march, it should have advanced guards and flanking parties, to examine well the country in front, to the right, and to the left, and always at such distance as to enable the main body to deploy into position.

8

A general-in-chief should ask himself frequently in the day: "What should I do if the enemy's army appeared now in my front, or on my right, or my left?" If he have any difficulty in answering these questions, his position is bad, and he should seek to remedy it.

9

The strength of an army, like the power in mechanics, is estimated by multiplying the mass by the rapidity; a rapid march augments the *morale* of an army, and increases its means of victory. Press on!

10

When an army is inferior in number, inferior in cavalry, and in artillery, it is essential to avoid a general action. The first deficiency should be supplied by rapidity of movement; the want of artillery, by the nature of the manœuvres; and the inferiority in cavalry, by the choice of positions. In such circumstances, the *morale* of the soldier does much.

11

To direct operations with lines far removed from each other, and without communications, is to commit a fault which always gives birth to a second. The detached column has only its orders for the first day. Its operations on the following day depend upon what may have happened to the main body. Thus, this column either loses time upon emergency, in waiting for orders, or it will act without them, and at hazard. Let it therefore be held as a principle, that an army should always keep its columns so united as to prevent the enemy from passing between them with impunity. Whenever, for particular reasons, this principle is departed from, the detached corps should be independent in their operations. They should move toward a point fixed upon for their future junction. They should advance without hesitating, and without waiting for fresh orders; and every precaution should be taken to prevent an attack upon them in detail.

12

An army ought to have only one line of operation. This should be preserved with care, and never abandoned but in the last extremity.

13

The distances permitted between corps of an army upon the march must be governed by the localities, by circumstances, and by the object in view.

14

Among mountains, a great number of positions are always to be found very strong in themselves, and which it is dangerous to attack. The character of this mode of warfare consists in occupying camps on the flanks or in the rear of the enemy, leaving him only the alternative of abandoning his position without fighting, to take up another in the rear, or to descend from it in order to attack you. In mountain warfare, the assailant has always the disadvantage; even in offensive warfare in the open field, the great secret consists in defensive combats, and in obliging the enemy to attack.

15

The first consideration with a general who offers battle, should be the glory and honor of his arms; the safety and preservation of his men is only the second; but it is in the enterprise and courage resulting from the former, that the latter will most assuredly be found. In a retreat, besides the honor of the army, the loss of life is often greater than in two battles. For this reason, we should never despair while brave men are to be found with their colors. It is by this means that we obtain victory, and deserve to obtain it.

16

It is an approved maxim in war, never to do what the enemy wishes you to do, for this reason alone, that he desires it. A field of battle, therefore, which he has previously studied and reconnoitred, should be avoided, and double care should be taken where he has had time to fortify and entrench. One consequence deducible from this principle is, never to attack a position in front which you can gain by turning.

17

In a war of march and maneuver, if you would avoid a battle with a superior army, it is necessary to entrench every night, and occupy a good defensive position. Those natural positions which are ordinarily met with, are not sufficient to protect an army against superior numbers without recourse to art.

18

A general of ordinary talent occupying a bad position, and surprised by a superior force, seeks his safety in retreat; but a great captain supplies all deficiencies by his courage, and marches boldly to meet the attack. By this means he disconcerts his adversary; and if the latter shows any irresolution in his movements, a skilful leader, profiting by his indecision, may even hope for victory, or at least employ the day in maneuvering—at night he entrenches himself, or falls back to a better position. By this determined conduct he maintains the honor of his arms, the first essential to all military superiority.

19

The transition from the defensive to the offensive is one of the most delicate operations.

20

It may be laid down as a principle, that the line of operation should not be abandoned; but it is one of the most skilful manœuvres in war, to know how to change it, when circumstances authorize or render this necessary. An army which changes skilfully its line of operation deceives the enemy, who becomes ignorant where to look for its rear, or upon what weak points it is assailable.

21

When an army carries with it a battering train, or large convoys of sick and wounded, it cannot march by too short a line upon its depôts.

22

The art of encamping in position is the same as taking up the line in order of battle in this position. To this end, the artillery should be advantageously placed, ground should be selected which is not commanded or liable to be turned, and, as far as possible, the guns should cover and command the surrounding country.

23

When you are occupying a position which the enemy threatens to surround, collect all your force immediately, and menace *him* with an offensive movement. By this maneuver, you will prevent him from detaching and annoying your flanks in case you should judge it necessary to retire.

24

Never lose sight of this maxim: that you should establish your cantonments at the most distant and best-protected point from the enemy, especially where a surprise is possible. By this means you will have time to unite all your forces before he can attack you.

25

When two armies are in order of battle, and one has to retire over a bridge, while the other has the circumference of the circle open, all the advantages are in favor of the latter. It is then a general should show boldness, strike a decided blow, and maneuver upon the flank of his enemy. The victory is in his hands.

26

It is contrary to all true principle, to make corps, which have no communication with each other, act separately against a central force whose communications are cut off.

27

When an army is driven from a first position, the retreating columns should rally always sufficiently in the rear, to prevent any interruption from the enemy. The greatest disaster that can happen, is when the columns are attacked in detail, and before their junction.

28

No force should be detached on the eve of a battle, because affairs may change during the night, either by the retreat of the enemy, or by the arrival of large reinforcements to enable him to resume the offensive, and counteract your previous arrangements.

29

When you have resolved to fight a battle, collect your whole force. Dispense with nothing. A single battalion sometimes decides the day.

30

Nothing is so rash or so contrary to principle, as to make a flank march before an army in position, especially when this army occupies heights at the foot of which you are forced to defile.

31

When you determine to risk a battle, reserve to yourself every possible chance of success, more particularly if you have to deal with an adversary of superior talent; for if you are beaten, even in the midst of your magazines and your communications, wo to the vanquished!

32

The duty of an advanced guard does not consist in advancing or retiring, but in maneuvering. An advanced guard should be composed of light cavalry, supported by a reserve of heavy cavalry, and by battalions of infantry, supported also by artillery. An advanced guard should consist of picked troops, and the general officers, officers and men, should be selected for their respective capabilities and knowledge. A corps deficient in instruction is only an embarrassment to an advanced guard.

33

It is contrary to the usages of war to allow parks or batteries of artillery to enter a defile, unless you hold the other extremity. In case of retreat, the guns will embarrass your movements and be lost. They should be left in position, under a sufficient escort, until you are master of the opening.

34

It should be laid down as a principle, never to leave intervals by which the enemy can penetrate between corps formed in order of battle, unless it be to draw him into a snare.

35

Encampments of the same army should always be formed so as to protect each other.

36

When the enemy's army is covered by a river, upon which he holds several *têtes de pont*, do not attack in front. This would divide your force and expose you to be turned. Approach the river in echelon of columns, in such a manner that the leading column shall be the only one the enemy can attack, without offering you his flank. In the meantime, let your light troops occupy the bank, and when you have decided on the point of passage, rush upon it and fling across your bridge. Observe that the point of passage should be always at a distance from the leading echelon, in order to deceive the enemy.

37

From the moment you are master of a position which commands the opposite bank, facilities are acquired for effecting the passage of the river; above all, if this position is sufficiently extensive to place upon it artillery in force. This advantage is diminished, if the river is more than three hundred toises (or six hundred yards) in breadth, because the distance being out of the range of grape, it is easy for the troops which defend the passage to line the bank and get under cover. Hence it follows that if the grenadiers, ordered to pass the river for the protection of the bridge, should reach the other side, they would be destroyed by the fire of the enemy; because his batteries, placed at the distance of two hundred toises from the landing, are capable of a most destructive effect, although removed above five hundred toises from the batteries of the crossing force. Thus the advantage of the artillery would be exclusively his. For the same reason, the passage is impracticable, unless you succeed in surprising the enemy, and are protected by an intermediate island, or, unless you are able to take advantage of an angle in the river, to establish a crossfire upon his works. In this case, the island or angle forms a natural *tête de pont*, and gives the advantage in artillery to the attacking army.

When a river is less than sixty toises (or one hundred and twenty yards) in breadth, and you have a post upon the other side, the troops which are thrown across derive such advantages from the protection of your artillery, that, however small the angle may be, it is impossible for the enemy to prevent the establishment of a bridge. In this case, the most skilful generals, when they have discovered the project of their adversary, and brought their own army to the point of crossing, usually content themselves with opposing the passage of the bridge, by forming a semicircle round its extremity, as round the opening of a defile, and removing to the distance of three or four hundred toises from the fire of the opposite side.

38

It is difficult to prevent an enemy, supplied with pontoons, from crossing a river. When the object of an army, which defends the passage, is to cover a siege, the moment the general has ascertained his inability to oppose the passage, he should take measures to arrive before the enemy, at an intermediate position between the river he defends and the place he desires to cover.

39

In the campaign of 1645, Turenne was attacked with his army before Philipsburg by a very superior force. There was no bridge here over the Rhine, but he took advantage of the ground between the river and the place to establish his camp. This should serve as a lesson to engineer officers, not merely in the construction of fortresses, but of *têtes de pont*. A space should always be left between the fortress and the river, where an army may form and rally without being obliged to throw itself into the place, and thereby compromise its security. An army retiring upon Mayence before a pursuing enemy, is necessarily compromised; for this reason, because it requires more than a day to pass the bridge, and because the lines of Cassel are too confined to admit an army to remain there without being blocked up. Two hundred toises should have been left between that place and the Rhine. It is essential that all *têtes de pont* before great rivers should be constructed upon this principle, otherwise they will prove a very inefficient assistance to protect the passage of a retreating army. *Têtes de pont*, as laid down in our schools, are of use only for small rivers, the passage of which is comparatively short.

40

Fortresses are equally useful in offensive and defensive warfare. It is true, they will not in themselves arrest an army, but they are an excellent means of retarding, embarrassing, weakening and annoying a victorious enemy.

41

There are only two ways of insuring the success of a siege. The first, to begin by beating the enemy's army employed to cover the place, forcing it out of the field, and throwing its remains beyond some great natural obstacle, such as a chain of mountains, or large river. Having accomplished this object, an army of observation should be placed behind the natural obstacle, until the trenches are finished and the place taken.

But if it be desired to take the place in presence of a relieving army, without risking a battle, then the whole *materiel* and equipment for a siege are necessary to begin with, together with ammunition and provisions for the presumed period of its duration, and also lines of contravallation and circumvallation, aided by all the localities of heights, woods, marshes and inundations.

Having no longer occasion to keep up communications with your depôts, it is now only requisite to hold in check the relieving army. For this purpose, an army of observation should be formed, whose business it is never to lose sight of that of the enemy, and which, while it effectually bars all access to the place, has always time enough to arrive upon his flanks or rear in case he should attempt to steal a march.

It is to be remembered, too, that by profiting judiciously by the lines of contravallation, a portion of the besieging army will always be available in giving battle to the approaching enemy.

Upon the same general principle, when a place is to be besieged in presence of an enemy's army, it is necessary to cover the siege by lines of *circumvallation*.

If the besieging force is of numerical strength enough (after leaving a corps before the place four times the amount of the garrison) to cope with the relieving army, it may remove more than one day's march from the place; but if it be inferior in numbers after providing for the siege, as above stated, it should remain only a short day's march from the spot, in order to fall back upon its lines, if necessary, or receive succor in case of attack.

If the investing corps and army of observation are only equal when united to the relieving force, the besieging army should remain entire within, or near its lines, and push the works and the siege with the greatest activity.

42

Feuquière says that "we should never wait for the enemy in the lines of circumvallation, but we should go out and attack him." He is in error. There is no authority in war without exception; and it would be dangerous to proscribe the principle of awaiting the enemy within the lines of circumvallation.

43

Those who proscribe lines of circumvallation, and all the assistance which the science of the engineer can afford, deprive themselves gratuitously of an auxiliary which is never injurious, almost always useful, and often indispensable. It must be admitted, at the same time, that the principles of field-fortification require improvement. This important branch of the art of war has made no progress since the time of the ancients. It is even inferior at this day to what it was two thousand years ago. Engineer officers should be encouraged in bringing this branch of their art to perfection, and in placing it upon a level with the rest.

44

If circumstances prevent a sufficient garrison being left to defend a fortified town, which contains an hospital and magazines, at least every means should be employed to secure the citadel against a *coup de main*.

45

A fortified place can only protect the garrison and detain the enemy for a certain time. When this time has elapsed, and the defenses of the place are destroyed, the garrison should lay down its arms. All civilized nations are agreed on this point, and there never has been an argument except with reference to the greater or less degree of defence which a governor is bound to make before he capitulates. At the same time, there are generals—Villars among the number—who are of opinion that a governor should never surrender, but that in the last extremity he should blow up the fortifications, and take advantage of the night to cut his way through the besieging army. Where he is unable to blow up the fortifications, he may always retire, they say, with his garrison, and save the men.

Officers who have adopted this line of conduct, have often brought off three-fourths of their garrison.

46

The keys of a fortress are well worth the retirement of the garrison, when it is resolved to yield only on those conditions. On this principle it is always wiser to grant an honorable capitulation to a garrison which has made a vigorous resistance, than to risk an assault.

47

Infantry, cavalry, and artillery, are nothing without each other; therefore, they should always be so disposed in cantonments as to assist each other in case of surprise.

48

The formation of infantry in line should be always in two ranks, because the length of the musket only admits of an effective fire in this formation. The discharge of the third rank is not only uncertain, but frequently dangerous to the ranks in its front. In drawing up infantry in two ranks, there should be a supernumerary behind every fourth or fifth file. A reserve should likewise be placed twenty-five paces in rear of each flank.

49

The practice of mixing small bodies of infantry and cavalry together is a bad one, and attended with many inconveniences. The cavalry loses its power of action. It becomes fettered in all its movements. Its energy is destroyed; even the infantry itself is compromised, for on the first movement of the cavalry it is left without support. The best mode of protecting cavalry is to cover its flank.

50

Charges of cavalry are equally useful at the beginning, the middle, and the end of a battle. They should be made always, if possible, on the flanks of the infantry, especially when the latter is engaged in front.

51

It is the business of cavalry to follow up the victory, and to prevent the beaten enemy from rallying.

52

Artillery is more essential to cavalry than to infantry, because cavalry has no fire for its defence, but depends upon the sabre. It is to remedy this deficiency that recourse has been had to horse-artillery. Cavalry, therefore, should never be without cannon, whether when attacking, rallying, or in position.

53

In march, or in position, the greater part of the artillery should be with the divisions of infantry and cavalry. The rest should be in reserve. Each gun should have with it three hundred rounds, without including the limber. This is about the complement for two battles.

54

Artillery should always be placed in the most advantageous positions, and as far in front of the line of cavalry and infantry as possible, without compromising the safety of the guns.

Field batteries should command the whole country round from the level of the platform. They should on no account be masked on the right and left, but have free range in every direction.

55

A General should never put his army into cantonments, when he has the means of collecting supplies of forage and provisions, and of thus providing for the wants of the soldier in the field.

56

A good general, a well-organized system, good instructions, and severe discipline, aided by effective establishments, will always make good troops, independently of the cause for which they fight.

At the same time, a love of country, a spirit of enthusiasm, a sense of national honor, and fanaticism, will operate upon young soldiers with advantage.

57

When a nation is without establishments and a military system, it is very difficult to organize an army.

58

The first qualification of a soldier is fortitude under fatigue and privation. Courage is only the second; hardship, poverty and want, are the best school for a soldier.

59

There are five things the soldier should never be without—his musket, his ammunition, his knapsack, his provisions (for at least four days), and his entrenching-tool. The knapsack may be reduced to the smallest size possible, if it be thought proper, but the soldier should always have it with him.

60

Every means should be taken to attach the soldier to his colors. This is best accomplished by showing consideration and respect to the old soldier. His pay likewise should increase with his length of service. It is the height of injustice not to pay a veteran more than a recruit.

61

It is not set speeches at the moment of battle that render soldiers brave. The veteran scarcely listens to them, and the recruit forgets them at the first discharge. If discourses and harangues are useful, it is during the campaign: to do away unfavorable impressions, to correct false reports, to keep alive a proper spirit in the camp, and to furnish materials and amusement for the bivouac. All printed orders of the day should keep in view these objects.

62

Tents are unfavorable to health. The soldier is best when he bivouacs, because he sleeps with his feet to the fire, which speedily dries the ground on which he lies. A few planks, or a little straw, shelter him from the wind.

On the other hand, tents are necessary for the superior officers, who have to write and to consult their maps. Tents should, therefore, be issued to these, with directions to them never to sleep in a house. Tents are always objects of observation to the enemy's staff. They afford information in regard to your numbers and the ground you occupy; while an army bivouacking in two or three lines, is only distinguishable from afar by the smoke which mingles with the clouds. It is impossible to count the number of the fires.

63

All information obtained from prisoners should be received with caution, and estimated at its real value. A soldier seldom sees anything beyond his company; and an officer can afford intelligence of little more than the position and movements of the division to which his regiment belongs. On this account, the general of an army should never depend upon the information derived from prisoners, unless it agrees with the reports received from the advanced guards, in reference to the position, etc., of the enemy.

64

Nothing is so important in war as an undivided command; for this reason, when war is carried on against a single power, there should be only one army, acting upon one base, and conducted by one chief.

65

The same consequences which have uniformly attended long discussions and councils of war, will follow at all times. They will terminate in the adoption of the worst course, which in war is always the most timid, or, if you will, the most prudent. The only true wisdom in a general is determined courage.

66

In war, the general alone can judge of certain arrangements. It depends on him alone to conquer difficulties by his own superior talents and resolution.

67

To authorize generals or other officers to lay down their arms in virtue of a particular capitulation, under any other circumstances than when they are composing the garrison of a fortress, affords a dangerous latitude. It is destructive of all military character in a nation to open such a door to the cowardly, the weak, or even to the misdirected brave. Great extremities require extraordinary resolution. The more obstinate the resistance of an army, the greater the chances of assistance or of success.

How many seeming impossibilities have been accomplished by men whose only resource was death!

68

There is no security for any sovereign, for any nation, or for any general, if officers are permitted to capitulate in the open field, and to lay down their arms in virtue of conditions favorable to the contracting party, but contrary to the interests of the army at large. To withdraw from danger, and thereby to involve their comrades in greater peril, is the height of cowardice. Such conduct should be proscribed, declared infamous, and made punishable with death. All generals, officers and soldiers, who capitulate in battle to save their own lives, should be decimated.

He who gives the order, and those who obey, are alike traitors, and deserve capital punishment.

❧ 69 ☙

There is but one honorable mode of becoming prisoner of war. That is, by being taken separately; by which is meant, by being cut off entirely, and when we can no longer make use of our arms. In this case, there can be no conditions, for honor can impose none. We yield to an irresistible necessity.

70

The conduct of a general in a conquered country is full of difficulties. If severe, he irritates and increases the number of his enemies. If lenient, he gives birth to expectations which only render the abuses and vexations, inseparable from war, the more intolerable. A victorious general must know how to employ severity, justice and mildness by turns, if he would allay sedition or prevent it.

71

Nothing can excuse a general who takes advantage of the knowledge acquired in the service of his country, to deliver up her frontier and her towns to foreigners. This is a crime reprobated by every principle of religion, morality and honor.

72

A general-in-chief has no right to shelter his mistakes in war under cover of his sovereign, or of a minister, when these are both distant from the scene of operation, and must consequently be either ill-informed or wholly ignorant of the actual state of things.

Hence, it follows, that every general is culpable who undertakes the execution of a plan which he considers faulty. It is his duty to represent his reasons, to insist upon a change of plan, in short, to give in his resignation, rather than allow himself to be made the instrument of his army's ruin. Every general-in-chief who fights a battle in consequence of superior orders, with the certainty of losing it, is equally blamable.

In this last-mentioned case, the general ought to

refuse obedience; because a blind obedience is due only to a military command given by a superior present on the spot at the moment of action. Being in possession of the real state of things, the superior has it then in his power to afford the necessary explanations to the person who executes his orders.

But supposing a general-in-chief to receive positive order from his sovereign, directing him to fight a battle, with the further injunction, to yield to his adversary, and allow himself to be defeated—ought he to obey it? No. If the general should be able to comprehend the meaning or utility of such an order, he should execute it; otherwise he should refuse to obey it.

73

The first qualification in a general-in-chief is a cool head—that is, a head which receives just impressions, and estimates things and objects at their real value. He must not allow himself to be elated by good news, or depressed by bad.

The impressions he receives either successively or simultaneously in the course of the day, should be so classed as to take up only the exact place in his mind which they deserve to occupy; since it is upon a just comparison and consideration of the weight due to different impressions, that the power of reasoning and of right judgment depends.

Some men are so physically and morally constituted as to see everything through a highly-colored medium. They raise up a picture in the mind on every slight occasion, and give to every trivial occurrence a dramatic interest. But whatever knowledge, or talent, or courage, or other good qualities such men may possess, nature has not formed them for the command of armies, or the direction of great military operations.

74

The leading qualifications which should distinguish an officer selected for the head of the staff, are, to know the country thoroughly; to be able to conduct a *reconnaissance* with skill; to superintend the transmission of orders promptly; to lay down the most complicated movements intelligibly, but in a few words, and with simplicity.

75

A commandant of artillery should understand well the general principles of each branch of the service, since he is called upon to supply arms and ammunition to the different corps of which it is composed. His correspondence with the commanding officers of artillery at the advanced posts, should put him in possession of all the movements of the army, and the disposition and management of the great park of artillery should depend upon this information.

76

The qualities which distinguish a good general of advanced posts, are, to reconnoitre accurately defiles and fords of every description; to provide guides that may be depended on; to interrogate the *curé* and postmaster; to establish rapidly a good understanding with the inhabitants; to send out spies; to intercept public and private letters; to translate and analyze their contents; in a word, to be able to answer every question of the general-in-chief, when he arrives with the whole army.

77

Generals-in-chief must be guided by their own experience, or their genius. Tactics, evolutions, the duties and knowledge of an engineer or artillery officer, may be learned in treatises, but the science of strategy is only to be acquired by experience, and by studying the campaigns of all the great captains.

Gustavus Adolphus, Turenne, and Frederick, as well as Alexander, Hannibal, and Cæsar, have all acted upon the same principles. These have been: to keep their forces united; to leave no weak part unguarded; to seize with rapidity on important points.

Such are the principles which lead to victory, and which, by inspiring terror at the reputation of your arms, will at once maintain fidelity and secure subjection.

78

Peruse again and again the campaigns of Alexander, Hannibal, Cæsar, Gustavus Adolphus, Turenne, Eugene, and Frederick. Model yourself upon them. This is the only means of becoming a great captain, and of acquiring the secret of the art of war. Your own genius will be enlightened and improved by this study, and you will learn to reject all maxims foreign to the principles of these great commanders.

Made in the USA
Monee, IL
06 July 2022